I0168509

THE
SEASONS
OF
LIFE

VICTOR DAUDA TARFA

Copyright © 2018 Victor Dauda Tarfa
Published by DVG STAR PUBLISHING
All rights reserved.
ISBN: 1-912547-15-5
ISBN-13: 978-1-912547-15-9

DEDICATION

To my beautiful wife Edna, who supported me
through all the seasons and inspired me to share my
experience with the world.
Thank you for believing in my dream, even when the
world thought you were crazy. Special thanks to my
lovely boys, David, Jotham, and Nathan who share
their dad with the world as he steps out to inspire
and transform a new generation.
I also dedicate this book to my family: Mum and
Dad, my sisters Victoria and Rejoice and brothers
Emmanuel, Joshua and Amos. My extended family
Mr and Mrs Tiya and Appollo, Sabina and Angela.

Love you all!

VICTOR DAUDA TARFA

CONTENTS

ACKNOWLEDGMENTS

I give God the glory for the tough times that made me understand the different seasons of life.
Big thanks to my wife and kids for their understanding when I lost all hope, and for helping me to revive my dreams and follow them as a bigger and better person.

For anyone that contributed in any way to this book, most importantly my mentor Ayo Ogundeji, thank you so much.

For you the reader, thanks a lot for taking the time to read my book.

"The biggest cause of frustration is standing still when we know we should be moving."

INTRODUCTION

Stuck in traffic, flight delayed or train coming to a standstill, causing you to be delayed? These can be very frustrating moments in life.

When we know there should be movement and we are at a standstill, or we want to make a move but do not know where or how to move, we lose all hope and frustration begins to kick in.

I had a great dream to transform the minds of young Nigerians because I was fed up with the state of the country. I had a choice, to either join in with the complaining or to focus and create a solution.

What solution can solve such a large problem with a nation of up to two hundred million people?

I looked for the root of the problem and realised that it was all down to how we think. If I could change their way of thinking, I could change their actions and that changes the results we see.

How do I spread the message and create the necessary impact? First I needed a medium to reach out, so I looked for opportunities to be invited to speak at events. I quickly realised if nobody knew me, I would not get an invite. I had to find a way to share my message so the world hears what I have to say, becomes interested and invites me.

I looked for what I had in my hand, social media and began to use it. I was not perfect but carried on.

One morning I got a call from a friend I had not spoken to in four years. He had seen my posts and videos on social media and was really inspired. He was interested in being a speaker too and wanted to know how to go about it.

I started to work on myself. I joined an organisation that taught me to speak and it created opportunities to practice in front of a crowd. I started to use social media to post inspirational messages and videos. These were platforms that were available to me to reach the world straight away.

It is about not playing the waiting game, it is about using the tools you have now to start. That phone call from my friend was a powerful trigger that showed results were already being created. It gave me the confidence to carry on. It was time to push harder to get my message of transformation out there. I need a stage, I thought.

"Do not hang around waiting for someone to invite you, you need to create your own party, show what you're made of and they will come looking for you."

This is some great and powerful advice from an experienced DJ speaking to a young lady on a television programme I was watching about a young lady who wanted to be a DJ. She went to see a more experienced DJ to teach her how to get into the crowded market and be heard. At that point, the penny dropped.

Armed with confidence and great advice, lots of personal development, coaching, and mentoring, I felt it was time I created my own platform. Now I knew I had a powerful message and the world needed to hear it, more people needed to be inspired to take action.

I created a platform called 'millionaires by forty', born out of a personal goal I set for myself. It was about encouraging young Africans to find their feet before the age of forty. As the saying goes, "life begins at forty".
I continued to spread the word through social media and seeking out people in the same field to learn from them.

As the saying goes, "if you look you will find". One day, I was looking through LinkedIn and an event popped out at me, being organised by a lady in Abuja, Nigeria, I noticed she had a large following so I reached out to her, built a relationship, took the big step, and planned a visit.

On arrival in Nigeria, I arranged a meeting and when I told her what I really wanted to do to create an event, she introduced me to an organisation that runs events in Nigeria. I reached out straight away to the owner and we arranged a meeting the same day.

When I met him we had so much in common, and most importantly we shared the same passion for young Nigerians and Africans. Soon as I told him about the kind of events I wanted to host, and he was excited and agreed to work with me.

Back in the UK I reached out to him and we set a date for the first event. It was my first public speaking gig, my first event, and I didn't have sponsors. How was I going to pay for the flights and hotels?

How do I contribute towards the venue and possibly other speakers? Fear, worry and everything scary you could think of gripped me. We set a date and I committed to it. I had to find a way to make it happen.
I have learned that once you set out committed to achieve a goal and get the confidence to start, it is amazing how the universe, nature, whatever you call your supernatural power, I call Him God He sends helpers and sponsors your way.

We had the event, and the organisation sponsored everything. All I did was turn up and I delivered my first speech. That was the beginning of a great journey.

I was invited back to speak at a female entrepreneurs event later in the year, and that also gave me the opportunity to meet and plan for the events for the next year.

I started the year seeking clarity on which way to take my mission and how to reach more people. I needed to plant more seeds in fresh ground and I needed clarity to seek where the best soil was.

One morning, I was sitting in quiet meditation and I heard a voice say "Go to Yola". Yola is the capital of Adamawa state, located in the northeast area of Nigeria.
It is my state of origin and since I had already had an event in the capital, Abuja, I needed to take on another Nigerian state.

I had spent a few years there while growing up. I had visited a few times but didn't really know enough people there to set up an event.
I had no idea where to start. I did not know any promoters, was not sure if any motivational events had been held there, and was totally unsure of the reception I was going to receive.

I started to make contacts, and I reached out to a friend I knew who lived there. He researched the best venue for me to use for the event and I secured it. The next step was how to do the publicity with a lack of promoters in the town.

It was a completely new idea; how could I explain it to the people so they could see the benefits of attending?

There is power in starting. Once we take the bold step, it is amazing all the help we get along the way. I was worried about getting people to attend the event and my mentor said to me "You can either be an earthquake or a termite". They can both cause damage to a building but at different levels and paces".
I went ahead with my plans with the mind-set that even if it was only one person that attended the event, I would still deliver like it was a full room.

It was a very successful event with a great turnout and the message was effective. I was invited on TV and radio shows as well as being invited to speak to the young people at a church. I went in as a termite but ended up an earthquake reaching far more people than I thought.

Months went by, and I was growing my network and relationships, and opening up more opportunities. I returned to Yola where we organised an event with a beauty queen who also shared a passion for the young people in the town.

I was also invited to Lagos, Southern Nigeria where I had the opportunity to share the stage with the best speakers and coaches in the country and also received an award in London for being an inspiration to the world. It was all go and I was loving it all but I was not getting paid. I was spending believing my payday will come. I focused on delivering value, building a strong brand and attracting opportunities.

I managed to drag myself out of bed, it was a cold and wet winter morning, all the kids were in school, my wife at work, I stood in the kitchen totally in thought, it was like my whole world had come crashing down, I had a deal I was so confident will change my fortune fall through, I was ill, went to see the consultant and he was concerned about my condition. Lots of blood tests and medication prescribed. It felt like the end of everything I had built.

I was totally caught in thought that the kettle had finished boiling and I didn't even notice. Everywhere was silent and then clearly I heard a voice say:

"Victor, why are you trying to sow seeds in your harvest season?"

I was invited back for a second time to speak at a young women leaders event in Abuja, Nigeria, we had agreed they would pay for my flights and hotels.

It was getting close to the time of the event and the logistics had not been sorted. I had promised to be there and the event had been advertised with me as a guest speaker. I had mentored some of the ladies in the past year, so they were excited that I was going to come back again. I felt that if I wasn't there I would be letting them down.

The organisers were let down by the sponsors, and there were all sorts of delays in the sponsoring of the event. It was looking like they were not going to be able to afford my flights and hotel. I decided I would pay for them myself. I was thinking, I need to sow seeds to eventually get my harvest.

In the past year I had sown so many seeds. My sisters heard about me travelling and were not happy that I was paying my way.

"How long will you keep sowing? It must be your harvest time by now."

So much was going through my mind; could this be the one last chance and they are holding me back from getting my needed break or are they seeing something I am not? I basically had hit a brick wall and was totally confused.

As I stood still in the kitchen, I heard that voice clearly, and I was totally set free. I had a flash back through the year and every stage of my journey was played back right in front of me, and I could clearly see all the seasons.

I understood the relationships, the tools that I used to get through each season, and how I moved on from one season to another. It was a total inspiration and I will be sharing the journey in this book.

In his book 'Man's Search for Meaning' Viktor E. Frankl wrote that we cannot give the true meaning of life based on a person's full lifetime, but by the meaning of the particular period they are in, at a particular time in a particular place.

This period in time can be referred to as a season. Our understanding of the meaning of every season helps us have the right tools to get through, have clarity of our mission on earth, and to know when to keep moving.

In this book, we would be looking at the different seasons of life, and investigating how to recognise them. We will discuss finding the right tools and learning from each season to help us move our lives to the next level.

CHAPTER 1
THE SEED

"Every great invention started from a small seed of thought."

That thought, little idea, that innovation, when sown and nurtured, can turn into a large invention.

Facebook started with a group of college students who just wanted to reach the people in their school.

Bill Gates started Microsoft in a little garage, Apple, formally known as Macintosh Computers, are all great inventions that came from very little ideas, which I will refer to here as seeds.

When I saw a problem, the state of my country, Nigeria, I looked at how I could create change. I got the idea, the seed, to create a movement to transform the mind-set of the younger generation.

We are all given seeds, the question is what we do with them. Some eat the seeds and that's the end of it, while some keep them and keep pondering on what to do with them, and after a long while they dry up and become useless.

Some plant the seeds, which is the highly recommended option. Unless a seed is planted there will never be a harvest.

When we receive a business idea, an innovation, or invention, it is like a seed. You need to find the right soil to plant it straight away; if not it is going to dry up and become useless. That's why so many ideas have not been brought to life, because when the seed was given it was left to rot and dry up.

Some people get frustrated because they held onto the idea for too long and when they decided to work on it, it was too late.

There are some key factors to consider when we get our seed:

a. The Good Soil:

>   Not all seeds grow in every kind of soil. Every plant needs a certain kind of soil to grow. Imagine if YouTube, the video streaming channel, was invented in the age of very slow internet connectivity.
>   It would have been very frustrating and would not have worked. It would have been the wrong soil to plant the seed and it would have just died. If I had tried to spread my message of transforming minds thirty-five to forty years ago in Nigeria, it would have been totally irrelevant because everything was working well at that time. We had a powerful currency and a great employment system. The seed's soil has to be correct.

b. Timing:

>   Have you ever had a great idea, but you didn't act on it then a few months later you see the product on the market?
>
>   We take a long time planning and looking for the perfect time to sow the seeds.

In the words of Mastin Kipp, "Take CIA: Courageous Imperfect Action".

Courage is the ability to take action even though you are absolutely scared. It does not mean the absence of fear. It is imperfect; just go with what you have.

The time is now. Don't wait for a perfect moment and action, make it happen, take that drastic step. Catapult yourself to a place of no return and you will have no choice but to keep going.

Time is a big factor with your seed.

Every idea dropped into our minds is very timely.

Speed of implementation is very important. We do not want that seed to dry up or go rotten.

The farmer can choose to preserve the seed but once the season for planting is past, they will have to wait for a long time for the opportunity to plant the seed again.

You need to plant it straight away.
There is always a strong reason why that idea dropped into your mind at that particular time. Execute the idea, don't wait!

c. Guard your seed:

If you plant a seed and do not build a fence around your garden, as soon as the plant begins to stick out, it will get eaten by pests. Some birds even dig out the seeds from the ground and eat them.

You need to be aware of the possible elements that could attack your seeds and be prepared to protect them.

You might be seen as crazy, or it may seem that the idea will not work, but you need to believe in your idea so much that even if nobody believes it's possible you still go for it.

Imagine the Wright brothers building a plane. It is hard to believe they could defy gravity but they stuck to the plan.

Henry Ford was told by his own engineers that they could not build the Ford car engine he wanted, but he stood his ground and it was built.

Everyone thought I was crazy when I talked about transforming the minds of nearly two hundred million people, one person at a time. I am making great progress.

You need to strongly believe in your seed, and hold on to that strong vision. If you don't nobody else will; after all, it's your idea.

When a farmer builds a fence around a plot of land, the land looks completely flat with no crops. If he's asked what he is doing and he says protecting his plants, everyone would think he is crazy.

All they can see is flat land, but the farmer sees large, fully grown plants. He sees an orchard with beautiful fruits. I can see a world where people take responsibility for their actions to help change the world in a positive way.

Now that you have your seed, you have got the right soil, the timing is right, you believe in it strongly and are willing to guard and protect it from the elements, the journey starts from planting to harvesting.

Different seeds take different times to grow, so we have to be patient and persevere. One guarantee is that as long as we have sown a seed there will always be a harvest. We just have to be willing to go through and understand the different seasons and then we can harvest our crop.

You also need to understand that whatever you are doing, whatever decisions you are making, and whatever actions you are taking, you are sowing a seed.

In the next chapters we will look at the different seasons of life up to our harvest.

"Life is a journey, along the way we encounter different situations I call seasons. Seasons cannot be avoided or altered. You can stand in the rain and complain about the fact it is raining, but that will not stop the rain. It is what you do that matters. Seasons will always come and go.

Some seasons last a long time, and some are very quick and they come as opportunities. The ability to recognise them, understand them and make the best of them is what really matters."

MY PERSONAL KEY LEARNING POINTS
FOR CHAPTER ONE

1.

2.

3.

4.

5.

"Insanity is doing the same thing over and over and expecting a different outcome!"

"BE THE CHANGE YOU WANT TO SEE."
– Mahatma Gandhi

I WILL ACT TODAY !

MY ONE ACTION POINT FOR TODAY !

CHAPTER 2
SEASON ONE

"Clarity: Having a clear destination, understanding it, and having a strong vision."

In Europe or America it is called winter. Dark, short days, heavy fog, and constant rain. In Nigeria where I grew up it is called 'Hammattan', dusty with poor visibility.

Whether you are in Europe or America or in Africa there is one common attribute to this season: poor visibility.

When I was in school in Lagos, Nigeria, we lived in Bauchi, which is in Northern Nigeria. During this season, every time I was returning to school we always had major flight delays because of poor visibility and thus the planes could not land.

Another major reason for the delays was because the planes did not have the necessary equipment and tools to land safely in this weather.

In this season the air and soil are extremely dry and thus the plants struggle to grow naturally.
It is certainly not the right time to plant your seed. When we go full circle, this is the season that comes after the harvest season and it is the time when the farmer puts out the crops that need to dry out in the sun.

When we get an idea, our seed, we feel so strongly about it but we are not sure how to go about realising it. We have the vision but due to a lack of full clarity and sometimes knowledge we struggle to see through all the obstacles on the way.

Just as the planes get delayed due to a lack of the right tools and equipment, we need the appropriate tools to get through this season.

a. Get a Coach/Mentor:

You cannot see the picture if you are in the frame. It is your idea and dream that you are very excited about.

It could be very difficult to see clearly. Also you might be limiting yourself because your emotions and excitement could take over and blur your vision.

A coach can help get all the ideas out of you so you can see beyond your emotions and excitement and see the reality of the seed. The coach will pull out all your potential, and they will help to stretch you properly to prepare you for the mission ahead. It could be daunting sometimes but well worth it.

A mentor will point you in the right direction. Usually this is someone that has walked in a similar path.

They can share their mistakes with you so you can avoid them and give you strategies for your ideas.

Your mentors could be physical people you spend time with or someone you follow on social media, someone whose books you read, blogs you follow, or videos you watch, etc. As long as they are in the same line as what you want to do, they are a good option.

When I started as a speaker, one of the first things I did was to get myself some support. I had one mentor I would meet with in person who really helped me gain clarity and I also had three virtual mentors: Les Brown, Mr Motivator, one of the biggest motivational speakers in the world; Bishop T.D Jakes. Pastor of the Porters House in Texas, USA; and Fela Durotoye, top Nigerian leadership coach/strategist and speaker, now a politician.

Each one of them played a significant role in my development. I watched their videos, listened to their audio products, attended their events and read their books.

So far I have met and spoken on stage with two of them, and the third is yet to come.

I was privileged to meet Les Brown and speak alongside him at the Global Women's

Conference in New York in July 2018. Fela Durotoye works in Nigeria and I have met him and spoken alongside him at a few events in Nigeria. He is like a personal friend to me now.

I have had the privilege to learn at the feet of Bishop TD Jakes in London and I am on the road to a meeting with him really soon.

These people started by mentoring me from afar, but because I put in the work, working with my physical mentors, I was able to grow and that created opportunities for me to meet and speak alongside my virtual mentors.

b. Personal Development:

This is one of the most important tools we all need in the seasons of life. Benjamin Franklin said "If you think education is expensive, try ignorance". One way we can keep developing our self is through education.

The more we study, attend events to learn from others, read books, and research, the more we grow our minds. This prepares us for the mission ahead.

The more you grow your mind, the more your perception of the things happening around you changes. You begin to see situations in a different light.

"The biggest investment you can make is not in property, gold or stocks and shares, it is in yourself.
That cannot be taken from you, it will never perish or lose value."

I believe personal development must be physical, mental and spiritual.

You need to exercise regularly to keep fit and heathy, and without good health you cannot grow your vision.

I started by training to run 5kms regularly and that has kept me in shape. I focus on discipline.
Morning runs discipline my mind. It is a strong way to prepare me mentally for the day.

Our mentality changes our way of thinking through studying and we begin to see the world differently, in a more positive way.
Reading books has drastically helped me grow mentally.
Spending time meditating and just listening for spiritual guidance goes a long way. It is very important to who you become, because if

you personally do not change you cannot change your situation or inspire others around you.

c. Relationships/Networks:

You desperately need to hang around the right people with the right mindset.

Avoid negative people like the plague.

If you want to become a speaker, there is no need to hang out at property investment meetings that teach you how to flip properties.
That is why clarity is important from the beginning because it will save you a lot of time and energy.
You have to choose the right meetings to go to and it is very important that you attend them with an intention and output in mind.

I used to randomly attend networking events and wasted so much of my time. I have learnt to be very systematic about it now.
Networking events give you an opportunity to talk about your vision with people. Sometimes you might be told it is not going to work, so find out why and use the reasons as a stepping stone and ammunition.

This prepares you for what is ahead. Also, having conversations helps you learn more about people's experiences with your competitors and are an opportunity to improve on that.

A great way to gather information is by talking to people about your vision. When I was planning to go to Nigeria to speak, I was attending various events I found out who the main speakers in Nigeria were and how to reach them. I eventually even spoke on the same stage with them in Lagos.

You have to understand that relationships and networks change as you go through different seasons. Some relationships might carry on all through your life but you need to know when to let go of some networks and people.

In conclusion to this chapter, just as a plane will not leave its location until the weather is clear enough for it to land at its destination or until it has the right tools and equipment to land, we need to have some understanding before we take off.

As we fly we need to make adjustments depending on the weather enroute, and most importantly we must have the right tools. Sometimes we might not have absolute clarity. When I started out I wanted to transform minds through speaking but didn't really know what topic to focus on. So, I got the right tools, took off, and now I'm writing this book.

You will not always have clarity at the beginning, but it is not an excuse not to start. Just take flight, you can always adjust along the way.

MY PERSONAL KEY LEARNING POINTS FOR CHAPTER TWO

1.

2.

3.

4.

5.

"Insanity is doing the same thing over and over and expecting a different outcome!"

"BE THE CHANGE YOU WANT TO SEE."
– Mahatma Gandhi

I WILL ACT TODAY !

MY ONE ACTION POINT FOR TODAY !

CHAPTER 3
SEASON TWO

"Unless a seed goes in the ground, it cannot reproduce."

You now have your seed, and you have some clarity on what to do with it.

As I said earlier, if it does not go in the ground, it will dry up and it's absolutely useless.
There cannot be a harvest unless the seed is sown. This is the Planting Season.

This is when action is taken and the process is started. This is the most important season.

The world is full of so many ideas, but most people never break through the barriers they create and get started. There are lots and lots of seeds in people's hands waiting to go in the soil.
But due to fear, lack of self-belief, procrastination, etc., the years have gone by and they are still holding onto them.

Stick your seed in the ground and watch it grow.

Every seed needs a certain type of soil to grow in, and the different types of soils are located in different areas of the world depending on the climate and current weather in the area.

Climate is the weather condition prevailing in an area in general or over a long period. The weather is the state of the atmosphere at a particular place and time.

Before we plant our seed we need to study the climate and weather of the area in which we are planting. When we take an idea we need to look at the current weather of the area, bearing in mind that weather is short term.

For example, if you are into clothing, you need to be selling summer clothing in the summer months.
If you take thick winter jackets to the market in the summer you will not sell many because it's hot and nobody needs them at that time.
Even though the climate, which is long term, gets cold, the weather, which is short term, is not right for that idea.

To make sure your seed grows effectively, you need the following key tools.

a. The right soil:

    Earlier I mentioned good soil.

    There is a difference between good soil and the right soil.
    You can have good soil but it might not be right for that particular seed you want to plant.

    You have to make sure the good soil is also the right soil to plant your seed.

    Rice grows best in swampy soil, maize in loamy soil without too much water, cocoa needs soil with a neutral to a very slightly acidic pH balance. These seeds are very choosy about their soil, to mention a few. In the same way, you need to make sure you know your market before heading in.

    I had to study who the motivational speakers in Nigeria were, how they operate, where they are located, who promotes them, how they get paid or who their sponsors are, who my audience is and so on before heading out there.

Knowing all this information helps with the strategy to plant your seed.

The soil is like the right business environment. The right idea in the right environment will certainly thrive.

b. The right location:

A seed needs to be planted in a location with easy access to the market.

It is pointless to plant a seed, nurture and grow it without access to your market.

If you create a software product for people that do not have access to computers then the seed has been planted in the wrong location.

No matter how great your idea is, if your customers cannot find you to benefit from the product it becomes a waste of time.

As you set out to plant your seed or idea always ask, am I in the right location to be spotted?

I see shops or restaurants in London located by traffic lights with nowhere for cars to stop and park for someone that wants to grab something quick, and this could affect a great business. Your location is very

important for your customers to find you
with ease.
That means the internet too.
Now we have different platforms like
Facebook, Instagram, Snapchat, LinkedIn
and many more. Make sure you are on the
right networks where your customers hang
out.

These two tools are very important for the planting
season.

The soil has to be right and the location of the crops
must have easy access to the market or visibility to
your target customers.

Another thing you need to understand about
planting is as a seed goes in the ground, dirt is
poured on top, and then it dies before it starts to
grow into a plant.

That means we have to plant with faith, believing
strongly the seed will grow. When you put it in the
ground, you cannot see the seed anymore, it just
takes faith and patience that at the appointed time
the plant will break through the soil and we begin to
see results.

When we start a business, sometimes we expect to
see immediate results, but in some cases we even
have to run at a loss, but because we believe so

much in our seed we keep watering it and waiting patiently and we will begin to see results.

We also need to understand that different seeds take different times to grow.

The bigger the tree the longer it will take because it needs to build a strong foundation, or roots, to support the plant or dream.

The bigger the dream the longer we need to work on the foundation.

MY PERSONAL KEY LEARNING POINTS
FOR CHAPTER THREE

1.

2.

3.

4.

5.

"Insanity is doing the same thing over and over and
expecting a different outcome!"

"BE THE CHANGE YOU WANT TO SEE."
– Mahatma Gandhi

I WILL ACT TODAY !

MY ONE ACTION POINT FOR TODAY !

CHAPTER 4
THE RAINY SEASON

"The rain is only a
nuisance to those
without seed in
the ground."

William McDowell

"Daddy, your phone is ringing", said my kids, who were playing a game on it while they waited their turn in the barber shop. I reached out and looked at who was calling, and answered it. It was a call I had been waiting for.

"Hi Victor, so sorry, it is not good news. The bank said they cannot do it".

I felt my legs grow weak and everything in me just sank. This deal was a game changer for me. It was the deal that was going to propel everything to the next level. I felt that it was taking me straight into my harvest as I waited to finalize it with the bank. I had thrown everything and more at it to make sure everything would pull through, but one small detail in valuation changed it all.

A week later I got a call from my doctor asking me to book an appointment to see him urgently. I had a blood test a few weeks ago and the results were in. "Victor, you look okay but your blood is telling me something else. We need to put you on some stronger medication because you are not well", the doctor said.

First my cash and now my health; I felt totally finished.

I travel around to speak and put on events, which needs finances.

Even if I had the money my health was not good, I couldn't travel and speak if I was sick, so I lost hope and that was like the final nail in the coffin. It was a very terrible time in my life.

You can lose everything, but once you lose the hope to even attempt to push back, that is the worst place to be. I could not see a way out, I lay in bed ill and hopeless.

My wife had never seen me like this. She tried to help but I said to her I just felt like Job from the Bible who lost everything including his health because he was being tested by the devil, but I forgot he never lost hope and when he bounced back, he was blessed with far more than he had before.

When we are in a dark place, the mistake we always make is to focus too much on the problem. I could remember Job's bad season but didn't remember the great result he had in the end.

Les Brown, one of the greatest motivational speakers, said "If you fall make sure you fall on your back because if you can look up you can get up". I fell face down.

"Surprise!", everyone screamed as I walked into the hall. It was Saturday afternoon, and I had been informed weeks earlier that we were invited to a wedding.

I made sure I had the day clear and I had to motivate myself to go out. I was feeling so down I did not even want to go out and meet people.

My wife told me she was one of the bridesmaids so she had to go out in the morning to help with arrangements, I was home with the kids all morning.

I struggled to finally get myself ready in the afternoon, all dressed to go to the wedding. We arrived at the venue late and did not want to disrupt events so decided to enter through the back door, and as I walked in it was the surprise of my life.

Even as I write this I still feel goose bumps because that was a major turnaround for me. When I looked through the hall in absolute disbelief, everyone that had been part of my life in different seasons were there to celebrate my 40th birthday with me. First I felt I didn't deserve all this, but I had to pull myself back and think of the lives I had touched so far with my seeds. I felt I deserved to be celebrated.
As humans we put ourselves down so much that even when we are appreciated we try to play it down.

We need to understand that as the labourer deserves his wages, we also deserve to be celebrated and appreciated for our contribution to the planet.

I totally could not believe my wife could plan and execute such a great party right under my nose without me having a single clue. I did not know anything was going on.

After the planting season comes the rainy season. It can be frustrating. It comes without warning: One minute you're walking around just fine and suddenly it pours down with rain and you are totally soaked.

Understanding the seasons goes a long way to having the right tools to pull through. You have a great seed, feel totally excited, plant it in the great soil, and then the rain comes. Imagine standing outside, it is raining heavily and you have no umbrella or raincoat; you were not prepared and did not expect the rain.

It could be a very frustrating experience. For a seed to grow it needs light, water and good soil. The natural way to water the seed is the rain.

The rainy season of life can be the toughest and so many people give up at this stage.
During this season we can become mistaken and begin to think maybe we were not supposed to be doing this, and it hurts badly. Les Brown said ,"We must always remember it's hard".

He spoke about the most important dream he had, to buy his mum a house. When he eventually did, he didn't do a proper inspection and he lost the house and a lot of money with it. Steve Jobs, the founder of Apple, was fired from the company he created.

The rain will always come, and we must learn how to get through those times with the right tools.

When it rains we get out the umbrella, the coat and we try to look for shelter to stay dry.

In business or life we get soaked and there is no escape there. With these tools we can keep going.

a. The right network:

As you build your business and dreams, I cannot emphasise enough the importance of having the right team of people around you. It is very important that you hold them very close and dear to you.

They are the only ones that will be left when it gets very tough. You will need all their encouragement. Be careful on your way up, and make sure everyone that truly shares your dream is carried along.

When it gets tough they share the pain with you and it is eased.

My wife could clearly see what I was going through, she knew I needed out and I lost hope.

When I said I felt like Job she knew she had to do something to cheer me up, and the birthday party was the solution. And it worked.

You have to make sure you build great relationships because you will certainly need them in the rainy season.

b. Strong values:

Les Brown said "If you don't stand for anything, you will fall for everything".

A lot of people fail and walk out in this season because they compromise their integrity when they are in pain and just want out.

When we are weak, we tend to be very prone to attack. All our guards are down and all sorts of ideas run through our minds.

We lose concentration but our values will always create boundaries and keep us focused. Personally I have four values I live by.

Any idea that runs through my mind or external suggestion I question it first.
- Responsibility; can I take full responsibility for the results it produces?
- Integrity; does it affect my integrity? Am I happy to put my name on it? Know that integrity is earned, and once lost it is tough to build again.
- Passion; do I feel passionate about the cause, does it align with what I am passionate about?

- Positive; is it positive? Will it produce a positive result? Will it have a positive impact on people or society?

Even when I am going to forward a message on social media I run through these values before I send it.

> I hold these values very close to my heart and I live by them all the time.
> Through tough times they help me stand firm and I do not compromise on my vision.
> I would strongly encourage you to create strong values and learn to stand by them all the time, whether you are being watched or not.

c. It will pass.

> Every season has a beginning and an end.

> No season will last forever, and the toughest of all the seasons is the rainy season. Knowing in our hearts that it will pass is the biggest consolation.

> The pain will pass.

> We have to keep being hopeful reminding ourselves and looking forward to the end and it will surely come.

This is the time where you must stand firm with the thought that if you give up, all the effort you have put in from the beginning will go to waste.

Stand firm! It will pass!

The tough times will surely come, the rain will get us absolutely soaked but stand firm with the right people and strong values around you, and it will pass.

The hard times create tenacity and build character, and character brings hope. Now you are ready for the next season.

MY PERSONAL KEY LEARNING POINTS FOR CHAPTER FOUR

1.

2.

3.

4.

5.

"Insanity is doing the same thing over and over and expecting a different outcome!"

"BE THE CHANGE YOU WANT TO SEE."
– Mahatma Gandhi

I WILL ACT TODAY !

MY ONE ACTION POINT FOR TODAY !

CHAPTER 5
THE HARVEST

"Every harvest starts with a seed."

"Victor, why are you sowing in your harvest season?" As I stood in my kitchen listening to the kettle boil, these words sounded clearly in my ears.

I was frustrated; it seemed like I had hit a dead end, and I was broke and sick. I was knocked down physically, mentally and spiritually.

It was time for me to move into my harvest and I was still planning a trip to sow more seeds.

The moment that happened, it was a turn around. Clearly it was harvest, but the question was, do I stand still and wait for the crops to come to me?

How do I differentiate between still sowing seeds and picking my harvest?

It is the year 2018, and I spent the whole of January meditating and planning my goals for the year. At the end of the month, I had all my goals written down with the travel plans and speaking engagements and events, as well as the one big event I would be planning in the year.

The month is now August and I have more than exceeded my goals. I have travelled to five large speaking engagements, and I visited three times more countries than planned in a short period, with many more planned for the rest of the year.

I have reached so many more people over social media and radio shows that I did not expect, and I am getting great feedback on how lives have been inspired and transformed.

It is my harvest season; it's time to rest and enjoy the fruit of my labour over the years, however it came with a lot more responsibility.

When you step into your harvest it is not a time to relax. It comes with a bigger responsibility; just like if the farmer left his crops and did not return to harvest, they would go rotten or could be eaten by animals or pests.

To get the best out of this season you have to have the right tools and principles.

a. You need to return to the farm:

When you sow seeds you must return to harvest them. Sometimes we get too impatient and keep moving from one idea to another.

We have to learn to stick to a plan, or in this case a plot of land and patiently wait for the harvest.

I was making a plan to travel to Nigeria. I had sown a lot of seeds in Yola, and I was planning to return to speak at an event there.

I was told you do not need to return there, it is only a small town and not much can come out of it. Because of the seeds sown there I knew I had a harvest.

Since I returned, I have been back there several times, and I have seen my influence grow massively there. I have had so many young people reach out to me with powerful inspiring stories, clearly the harvest was ripe there.

No matter how irrelevant a location might have looked on your journey, it will definitely have played a great role in your success.

Look closely, there is a harvest there.

b. Gather your harvest and prepare for the market:

When a farmer returns to his farm for the harvest, he needs to gather all the crops and prepare them for market.

In the earlier chapter, I mentioned the importance of clarity.

You need to establish a clear outcome. When you plant crops, you must know what you want to do with it, who you want to sell it to, and where your market is.

Sometimes the market conditions might change, but you need to be aware and adjust accordingly.

Most importantly, you need to know what you want to do with the crop so you know how to harvest it and prepare it for market.

This is when you start to leverage the relationships you have built along the way, and the learnings from the rainy season. You become very busy now because people begin to reach out to you, and all the hard work begins to pay off. It is certainly not a time to relax or rest, it is a time when things get really busy and you need to be prepared for the multiple opportunities that will come your way. Some will be planned, some come at the last minute.

I have just spent a month where I was hardly in the country, I was on a stage every weekend, and on a radio station that reaches up to a million people in one country. I never expected that I was going to inspire that many in a month.

That is what the harvest is all about.

c. The product:

As a cocoa farmer the final product is chocolate, as a cotton farmer it will be linen or as a wheat farmer it will be bread; there is always a final product.

You might not be a manufacturer of the final product but your products set the transformation in motion.

I am a Transformational Speaker, and my focus is to inspire and transform. This book is one of my products. I may not see the final transformation physically, but I know what I am aiming to achieve and that's why I wrote this book.

You will need to create a product so as to fully reap your harvest.

MY PERSONAL KEY LEARNING POINTS FOR CHAPTER FIVE

1.

2.

3.

4.

5.

"Insanity is doing the same thing over and over and
expecting a different outcome!"

"BE THE CHANGE YOU WANT TO SEE."
– Mahatma Gandhi

I WILL ACT TODAY !

MY ONE ACTION POINT FOR TODAY !

CHAPTER 6
FULFILLMENT THE NEW CURRENCY

"Success without fulfilment is the ultimate failure." Tony Robbins

One very common affirmation we hear all the time, especially at the beginning of the year, is "This is my year of harvest".

The question is "Have you sown a seed?"
If yes, "What kind of seed have you sown?"

We need to understand that not every seed sown is a good seed, and one guarantee is whatever you sow you will reap.

If you declare your time of harvest, you will need to be sure you have sown a good seed. If not you are bringing a curse upon yourself. The better your seed is, the more your fruit will reach the world.

As I heard the words clearly, "Victor, why are you sowing in your harvest season?", the whole year flashed back at me. It was definitely clear that I needed that shift.
It was like a miracle had been activated. My crop was ripe and I had to harvest it.

This might sound or feel like the work is all done now and it is time to relax and get the harvest in, but I am sorry to say, there is still a lot of work to be done.
Sometimes it even gets harder because the responsibilities increase and a lot more people are depending on you.

In business this could be a period where your business starts to expand massively. You now have a lot of employees and their families depending on you, and it might look like you have gone back to the rainy season. But it is a great feeling of fulfilment because right before your eyes are the results of all the hard work.

You have survived the rain, and now you are unstoppable and ready for bigger problems.

Fulfilment is now the new currency. Most people think once it is harvest, lots of money will begin to flow into their bank accounts.

Yes money will come, but most importantly focus on fulfilment.

How many lives have you positively transformed? How does your life inspire others? Are you operating on your full potential and being of great service to the world?

Imagine as an estate agent the joy and smile on the customer's face when they settle into the home of their dreams, a taxi driver glad to see every customer dropped off at their destination safely or a traffic warden happy to see traffic moving freely because everyone is considerate and has parked in the right places, not blocking the roads.

The estate agent is not focusing on how to squeeze as much commission as possible from the family, a taxi driver is not thinking of the longest route so as to get as much money as possible and the traffic warden not focusing on the promotion he gets for the number of tickets issued.

I really hope that, as you read this book, spend time reflecting on what truly makes you happy, and what makes you feel fulfilled.

We need to realise we are all here to serve, and true happiness will only come through by sowing the right seeds, nurturing them through the process, harvesting and spreading the fruits out in the world.

We also have to remember you need to keep some seeds so as to replant for the next year.

MY PERSONAL KEY LEARNING POINTS FOR CHAPTER SIX

1.

2.

3.

4.

5.

"Insanity is doing the same thing over and over and expecting a different outcome!"

"BE THE CHANGE YOU WANT TO SEE."
– Mahatma Gandhi

I WILL ACT TODAY !

MY ONE ACTION POINT FOR TODAY !

"The pessimist sees difficulty in every opportunity. The optimist sees opportunity in every difficulty." Winston Churchill

CHAPTER 7
GRATITUDE

"Gratitude makes sense of our past, brings peace for today, and creates a vision for tomorrow."
Melody Beattie

You have received a large harvest after all your hard work.
Looking at it, you might be feeling you have been short changed and deserved a lot more.

As important as it is to be aware of where you are in your journey and have the right tools, you must learn the appropriate lesson and prepare to move on.

You must be grateful and appreciate where you are to move on. As the great book, the Bible, says "Give thanks in every situation". On my journey I have learnt to be grateful all the way.

No matter how tough it gets there is always something to be grateful for.

Gratitude is the major key to happiness.

We need to understand that gratitude is not an opportunity to live a mediocre life.

I see people living below their potential. They are overweight, they do not have money, they are in a dead end job, they know they need to move on but do not have the courage to do so, to take action and start again.

When they are challenged they say "I am happy", but clearly you can see they are not, sadly they just don't want to move out of their comfort zone. Maybe they have tried but they think it's crazy or people have called them crazy. Bernard Buchard says, "If you have never been called crazy, you are not operating outside limits. You are sitting comfortably in your comfort zone.

Being grateful is when you know you have done your best, operated to total capacity, you have pushed yourself to the exceptional limit, and you see the results you create, and you have every reason to be grateful.

True happiness comes from being happy with yourself and appreciating your location and being grateful.

I make sure I keep a gratitude journal every day. I have learnt to write down something I am grateful for every day.

Whatever situation I find myself I focus on the positive side. There always is one.

What are you grateful for? Focus on the positives and you will find true happiness.

WHAT ARE YOU GRATEFUL FOR?

1.

2.

3.

4.

5.

6.

7.

8.

"Gratitude is not only the greatest of virtues, but the parent of all others."

Marcus Tullius Cicero

CHAPTER 8
HOW TO ACHIEVE YOUR GOALS AND DREAMS

Have you ever entered a marathon race before? The process of generally enrolling and training is usually very tedious and mentally strenuous. Still, you feel a lot of joy when you eventually go on to win the race. The same can be said about the process of achieving your goals. The process is one which is detailed and should be followed promptly. I do a 5km run every morning with the exception of Sundays, I love the final feeling when the run is over, I love to look at the results when I beat the last record, but I hate the process because it is tough. What keeps me going is the thought of the result and I have grown to love the process.

The process is not going to be easy, just focus on the results you want to create.

Identify your goals and dreams: You cannot begin to chase after another person's dreams, and that is the reason why you need to identify what you want to become.

Learn: The process of learning is the period where you conduct research to identify mentors in your career path and also make a consistent effort to learn from them. No one is an island of their own and that is why you need to learn from others. You can begin to learn from various other books. Search for books that are within your career path and ensure that you read and meditate on them.

Focus: The process of achieving your goals requires your intense focus as there is absolutely nothing you can achieve if you are not focused. When you fix your focus on what you desire, it draws closer to you because your focus is like a magnet. This also involves knowing exactly what you want to achieve, that way you acquire the correct tools for the job.

My youngest son had an assignment to complete, he said he needed some things from an art shop. I took him out there. He kept on walking round the shop not knowing what to pick. Because he didn't know what he wanted to make in the first place, he didn't know what materials he needed. We ended up leaving without buying anything.

Focus, know clearly what you want to achieve, get the right tools and you will succeed.

Action: Action is needed if you are ever going to reach the top, because no one can afford to keep learning without taking the first step. We live in a world with many people talking about what they want to do, years later it is still not done. Lots of talk no action.

As you finish this book, I will love to hear your story of how you have taken action with the information you have acquired.

"You learn more from failure than from success. Don't let it stop you. Failure builds character."
Unknown

CHAPTER 9
HOW TO ACHIEVE WORK-LIFE BALANCE

We all have great dreams, goals and aspirations. We have mega things we want to do and change the world. One thing that separates the successful from those that don't succeed is who is willing to put in the hard work.

A lot of people start, when it gets too hard, they walk away. They are not willing to stretch. It involves hard work, you have to create a balance.

I get asked all the time, You are a husband, father of three boys, International Transformational Speaker, Corporate MC, Coach how do you do all that effectively? It's all about being intentional about creating a balance and knowing there is time for everything.

Be Intentional: You need to recognize the need to bond with your family, chances are high that you will not create any time for them.
You need to start from when they are in the belly. I attended every scan with my wife and made sure I was present at all the birth of my boys. I totally understood the importance of creating a strong bond. Because I have created that bond, even when I need to travel for long, we still maintain the love because of the strong foundation.
I have also attend almost 100 percent of their school activities, its makes such a massive difference to them when I do that.

I returned from speaking in Nigeria, just arrived from the airport, I went straight to their activity without even going home. I am very intentional about being around and when I am around I make sure I am present. No phone distractions, I focus on them.

The key is knowing the importance and making the effort.

Plan: In order to achieve a balanced life, you should draft a schedule that your work and life activities can fit into. Such schedules can be drawn in hours or days and within it, you should create times to go out with friends as well as be alone with family. Schedule holidays with the whole family and with just your spouse. Get someone to look after the kids and date nights. When we had kids, we didn't go out for a while because we worried about childcare, now I don't worry anymore since I discovered the importance, we just pay for a nanny and go out when necessary. Plan special times, schedule them and even if business comes in your way, you really have to have a strong reason to move it. You must attach a lot of importance to your family. As I wrote earlies, when I went through my rainy season my wife help me pull through. If I had ignored her earlier, she would not have been there for me.

Be Spontaneous: This might sound crazy, earlier I said plan, now I say be spontaneous.

It is great to create moments and one way of doing that is being spontaneous. Turn up un announced and take your spouse to lunch, driving home with the kids, just drop in for a snack in a fast food restaurant. Come up with ideas and keep creating surprises. Break out of routine and create time for them. Leave the office early, go later than planned and drop the kids at school first. Remember great memories matter.

Most people who value work over every other activity are often very rigid and this impedes them from achieving balance. You should learn to break out from your routine to create time for loved ones.

"It's not whether you get knocked down, it's whether you get up."

Vince Lombardi

CHAPTER 10
KEY QUOTES

"The bigger the dream, the harder and longer you will need to work."

VICTOR DAUDA TARFA

"Don't worry about the 'How', once you commit, you will find a way."

92

"Any decision or action you take, you are sowing a seed."

"It takes every seed a different amount of time to grow depending on the weather, location and how well the farmer looks after it. Everyone's season is different. Don't go comparing."

"The grass looks greener on the other side; it's the hard work that was invested to make it flourish."

NOTES TO THE READER

Thank you for investing your time in reading my book.

KNOWLEDGE IS NOT POWER!

ONLY ACTIVE KNOWLEDGE IS POWER!

TAKE ACTION EACH AND EVERY DAY – THE JOURNEY OF A THOUSAND MILES BEGINS WITH ONE STEP.

TAKE DAILY ACTION AND MAKE YOUR GOALS AND DREAMS COME TRUE.

With love and blessings for your success,

Victor Dauda Tarfa

"The future belongs to the competent. Get good, get better, be the best!"

Success quote by Brian Tracy

VICTOR DAUDA TARFA

ABOUT THE AUTHOR

Victor Dauda Tarfa is an international transformational speaker, mentor, corporate MC and seasons coach.

He is the founder of "The Victor", a transformational network with a vision to inspire a new generation to take responsibility and create the future they want to see.

Born in the United Kingdom, he grew up in his native country Nigeria. He later returned to the UK, but he was not happy with the state of his native country.

He set out to transform people's way of thinking, because he believes that if we can change the way we think, we can change the way we act and we can change the results we create.

Victor vowed to do something about the situation by organising transformational events. With his powerful transformational words, he leaves an impact in the minds of people all over the world, completely transforming their lives.

From sowing seeds in Nigeria, his fruits have spread stages around Africa, Europe and the United States. He has shared stages with world class speakers like the likes of Les Brown and other renowned world class speakers.

Victor has also been interviewed on TV and radio stations worldwide.

You can connect with me on social media Facebook, Instagram and LinkedIn. Search for Victor Dauda Tarfa will love to hear from you.

PERSONAL NOTES:

PERSONAL NOTES:

PERSONAL NOTES:

www.ingramcontent.com/pod-product-compliance
Lightning Source LLC
Chambersburg PA
CBHW031141090426
42738CB00008B/1181